DIVINE DESSERTS

A Taste of Indulgence

DIVINE DESSERTS

MARGARET O'SULLIVAN

LONGMEADOW PRESS

Copyright © 1995: Lansdowne Publishing Pty Ltd
Copyright design © 1995: Lansdowne Publishing Pty Ltd

Published by Longmeadow Press 1996
201 High Ridge Road, Stamford, CT 06904

Produced by Lansdowne Publishing Pty Ltd
Level 5, 70 George Street, Sydney 2000, Australia

Design: Modern Times Pty Ltd
Photographer: André Martin
Stylist: Donna Hay
Typeset in Garamond on Pagemaker

ISBN 0-681-10538-0

Printed in Singapore by Kyodo Printing Co. Pte

First Longmeadow Press Edition

0 9 8 7 6 5 4 3 2 1

Front cover: Rasberry Chocolate Cups, recipe page 89
Page 2: Panforte with Chantilly Cream, recipe page 75
Back cover: Cherry Clafouti, recipe page 29

Contents

Introduction

DESSERT can transform an ordinary meal into a sublime indulgence. We eat dessert purely for pleasure, and that faint aura of forbidden fruit enhances our enjoyment. Divinely decadent chocolate confections, light-as-air soufflés, melting meringues, perfect profiteroles — we may not eat them for our health, but they certainly increase our happiness and sense of well being.

The origin of dessert is lost in the mists of time, but we can thank the ancient Greeks for inventing pastry — and probably the plum pudding. The tradition of eating something sweet at the end of a meal certainly goes back a long way.

When deprived by dieting it's the sweet treats we miss most. Let's face it, the comfort factor simply isn't there in low energy foods. Most of us don't eat dessert every day, but when we do it should be something scrumptious.

More than any other food, desserts stir our imagination — and our creativity in the kitchen. A homemade dish is always a compliment to guests because it shows the occasion is special. Store-bought desserts just don't taste the same — nor is it possible to buy many of the most truly delectable desserts.

This doesn't mean that you have to spend hours slaving in the kitchen. A homemade dessert need not look like a dish prepared by a restaurant chef, although you can often achieve the effect without a lot of hard work. But the appeal of some desserts lies in their homemade quality, which triggers happy memories of childhood treats.

All of the recipes in this book are easy to make and require no special skills.

Some of my personal favorites, for instance, Cointreau Ice-cream (page 43) and Strawberries Jellied in Red Wine (page 97), are simple to make, yet they could feature on any top restaurant menu.

At banquets in 18th century France, dessert followed at least four other courses and was always served after the cheese. It was presented in truly magnificent style. At the beginning of the meal large decorative sculptures made of pastry were placed on the table with baskets of fruit arranged in pyramids. Incidentally, you weren't allowed to nibble the sculptures. When it was time for dessert, an array of sweets would be elegantly arranged in accordance with a detailed plan so that they harmonized with the gold plate and crystal.

Presentation is still important. At dinner parties I like to serve dessert at the table — somehow the effect is more bounteous. Clear any condiments relating to previous courses, but return any fruit or flower arrangements that have been removed so that the table looks as decorative as possible. Nowadays dessert can be served before or after cheese. In some cases (if dessert is not hot, or likely to melt) it's possible to put both on the table together and let guests decide for themselves. And if you plan to serve chocolates or petits fours with coffee, you can bring them out too at this stage — it all adds to a bountiful effect. Whether to serve a dessert wine or continue with what you've been drinking is up to you, but remember: red wine and chocolate are incompatible.

While, for many of us, dessert is the highlight of the meal it nevertheless has to work with the other courses. Each element of a meal has to fit together to enhance the others.

Try not to have too much of a good thing. Don't follow a rich, creamy main course with a rich, creamy dessert. Or if you serve figs with prosciutto as a first course, don't make fruit the finale. A coconut flavored dessert can be a fitting end to an Asian meal, but not if coconut cream has been used in any of the main course dishes. If eggs have been incorporated in other courses, for instance in Bernaise Sauce, don't serve an egg custard or a soufflé.

If the main course is light and simple, for instance, seafood and salad, take the opportunity to finish with something rich. But try to follow heavy food with a light dessert. The season is also important: fruit ices are wonderful in summer, but don't offer much comfort on a cold night. Heavier puddings and pastries are best in cooler weather, and some chocolate desserts aren't suited to summer because of their tendency to melt.

Desserts sweeten our lives. Fads come and go, but the tradition of ending a meal on a sweet note is here to stay.

THE RECIPES

Amaretto Jelly

2 packets (5 oz/150 g) raspberry jelly
    crystals
3 cups (26 fl oz/800 ml) boiling
    water
4 oz (125 g) berries – strawberries,
blueberries, raspberries

½ cup (2 fl oz/60 ml) Amaretto
    (almond liqueur)
berries, extra

A SIMPLE fruit jelly is transformed by the addition of Amaretto (almond
liqueur).

Dissolve the jelly crystals in the boiling water in a saucepan. Add the
berries, bring the liquid rapidly to simmering point and poach for
1 minute. Add the Amaretto and stir.

Pour into individual molds. Try to distribute the berries evenly —
they will tend to bob to the surface, but this won't matter when the jelly is
turned out. Put the jellies into the refrigerator to set.

When ready to serve, turn the jellies out and decorate with fresh
berries.

Serves 6

Apple Pie

1 lb (500 g) canned pie apples

2 tablespoons packed (soft) brown
  sugar

1 teaspoon cinnamon

½ teaspoon nutmeg

grated peel (rind) of 1 lemon

8 oz (250 g) ready rolled shortcrust
  pastry

8 oz (250 g) ready rolled puff pastry

1 egg, beaten

superfine (caster) sugar

A COMBINATION of shortcrust pastry underneath the filling, and puff pastry on top, makes a great apple pie that is brilliant served with shavings of top quality Parmesan (or any other cheese you fancy).

Chop the canned pie apples into small pieces and mix with the brown sugar, cinnamon, nutmeg and grated lemon peel.

On a floured board cut one piece of shortcrust pastry and one piece of puff pastry to fit a 10 inch (25 cm) circular pie plate. Lightly grease the pie plate and line it with the shortcrust pastry. Fill with the apple mixture. Top the pie plate with the remaining piece of puff pastry. Using a star-shaped cookie cutter, cut star shapes from leftover puff pastry and decorate the top of the pie. Crimp the edges to seal and cut two small slits in the top to allow steam to escape.

Brush the pastry with beaten egg and sprinkle with superfine sugar.

Bake in a very hot oven (450°F/230°C/Gas Mark 8) for 10 minutes, then reduce heat to moderate (350°F/180°C/Gas Mark 4) and continue cooking for about 30 minutes longer, until golden brown.

Serves 6

Baked Ricotta Cheesecake

BASE
6 oz (180 g) plain sweet crackers
1 cup (3 oz/90 g) unsweetened
    (desiccated) coconut
4 oz (125 g) butter, melted
FILLING
4 eggs
1 cup (8 oz/250 g) sugar

juice and grated peel (rind) of
    2 lemons
1 lb (500 g) ricotta cheese
2 oz (60 g) blanched almonds,
    chopped
Praline, for serving
heavy (double) cream, for serving

TO MAKE the base, process the crackers and coconut in a food processor or blender until finely ground. Transfer to a bowl and combine with the melted butter. Press into the base of a greased 10 inch (25 cm) springform pan and refrigerate until firm.

To make the filling, beat the eggs in a bowl until light and frothy. Gradually beat in the sugar, then the lemon juice and peel.

In a separate bowl combine the ricotta cheese and the blanched almonds. Stir the egg and lemon mixture gradually into the ricotta.

Pour the filling over the prepared base and bake in a moderately hot oven (375°F/190°C/Gas Mark 5) for 40 minutes, or until set. Cool in the pan. To serve, decorate with cream and Praline.

Serves 8

PRALINE

•

1 cup (4 oz /125 g) sugar

2 tablespoons water

1 teaspoon fresh lemon
juice

2 oz (60 g) almonds,
toasted and sliced

•

Combine the sugar, water and lemon juice over a low heat and swirl until sugar dissolves. Do not stir. Increase the heat to medium high and boil until the syrup just caramelizes. Stir almonds into caramel and immediately pour mixture into a well-oiled baking pan. Cool until hardened. Break into small chunks.

•

Banana and Passionfruit Cheesecake

CRUST

8 oz (250 g) plain sweet crackers,
    crushed
½ teaspoon nutmeg
½ teaspoon cinnamon
4 oz (125 g) butter, melted

FILLING

4 teaspoons gelatin
½ cup (4 fl oz/125 ml) water

8 oz (250 g) cream cheese
1 cup (8 oz/250 g) sugar
grated peel (rind) of 1 lemon
¼ cup (2 fl oz/60 ml) lemon juice
1⅔ cups (14 fl oz/450 ml)
    evaporated milk, chilled
1 banana, for serving
lemon juice, extra for serving
Passionfruit Topping, for serving

COMBINE all of the crust ingredients in a bowl and press into the sides and base of a greased 8 inch (20 cm) springform pan.

To make the filling, put the gelatin in the water and stir over hot water to dissolve. Set aside to cool. Beat the cream cheese and sugar together until smooth. Add the lemon peel and juice, and the dissolved gelatin. Combine well. Refrigerate until partially set.

Whip the evaporated milk in a chilled bowl until soft peaks form. Add to the cream cheese mixture. Pour the mixture into the crust. Refrigerate overnight or until set.

To serve, decorate with slices of banana that have been brushed with the extra lemon juice and pour over the Passionfruit Topping.

Serves 8

PASSIONFRUIT TOPPING

•

½ cup (4 fl oz/125 ml)
lemon juice
pulp of 2 passionfruit
2 tablespoons sugar
3 teaspoons cornstarch
(cornflour)

•

Put the lemon juice, passionfruit pulp and sugar into a saucepan and bring to simmering point. Mix the cornstarch with a small amount of water to make a paste and add to the saucepan. Continue cooking over a low heat, stirring constantly, until the mixture thickens. Cool and refrigerate.

•

Banana Bundles

24 sheets filo pastry
6 oz (180 g) butter, melted
6 small ripe bananas, peeled

4 oz (125 g) macadamia nuts,
 chopped
Caramel Sauce, for serving

TAKE the sheets of filo pastry and cut in half so that you have roughly square sheets. Put four squares together, brush each square with melted butter and top with a roughly chopped banana.

Brush the banana with melted butter, sprinkle with some of the macadamia nuts and gather the filo into a bundle, fanning out the pastry at the top.

Loosely tie with kitchen string to secure the bundles. Repeat with the remaining bananas.

Bake in a moderately hot oven (375°F/190°C/Gas Mark 5) for about 25 minutes or until golden brown. Remove the string. Serve with Caramel Sauce and icecream.

Serves 6

CARAMEL SAUCE

•

6 oz (180 g) sugar
¾ cup (6 fl oz/180 ml) water
1¼ cups (10 fl oz/300 ml) heavy (double) cream

•

Put the sugar and water into a saucepan and stir over medium heat until the sugar dissolves. Bring to simmering point and cook without stirring until golden. Remove from the heat and leave for a minute, then add the cream and stir. To serve, warm over a low heat but do not boil.

•

Banana Cream Wafers

4 oz (125 g) butter, softened
6 oz (180 g) superfine (caster) sugar
¼ cup (1 fl oz/30 ml) maple syrup
3 oz (90 g) all-purpose (plain) flour

2 egg whites
Banana Cream, for serving
bananas, for serving

CREAM the butter and sugar until light and fluffy. Beat the egg whites until soft peaks form. Stir the maple syrup and flour into the butter and sugar, then fold in the egg whites.

Line two baking sheets with parchment (baking paper) and drop spoonfuls of the mixture onto the trays, leaving room in between for the mixture to spread to wafer thinness (about 3 inches/7.5 cm across). (Note: If the mixture does run together during cooking, cut into serving pieces when cool.)

Bake in a moderate oven (350°F/180°C/Gas Mark 4) for 15–20 minutes until golden brown. Leave to cool on the baking sheets for about 1 minute, then use an egg lifter to transfer the wafers to a wire rack.

When cool, store in an airtight container.

Just before serving sandwich with the Banana Cream and sliced banana.

Makes about 20 wafers

BANANA CREAM

•

1¼ cups (10 fl oz/300 ml) heavy (double) cream

•

3 bananas

•

Make this just before serving. Whip the cream until soft peaks form. Mash the bananas well, then fold into the cream. NOTE: You can substitute thick honey yogurt for the whipped cream if desired.

•

Bread Cake

6 eggs, separated
1 cup (8 oz/250 g) sugar
1 ¼ cups (2 oz/60 g) dry
    breadcrumbs
½ teaspoon double-acting baking
    powder (1 teaspoon baking
    powder)
1 teaspoon cinnamon
grated peel (rind) of 1 orange
½ cup (2 fl oz/60 ml) orange juice

1 cup (5 oz/150 g) blanched
    almonds, ground finely
SHERRY SYRUP:
¾ cup (6 fl oz/180 ml) dry sherry
2 tablespoons brandy
¼ cup (2 oz/60 g) sugar
2 cloves
1 strip orange peel (rind)
Toffee Bark (page 27), for serving
heavy (double) cream, for serving

PUT THE egg yolks in a food processor or blender then add the sugar gradually while processing. Add the remaining ingredients except the egg whites and process briefly to combine.

In another bowl beat the egg whites until soft peaks form. Fold the mixture from the food processor lightly into the egg whites. Scrape the mixture into a 9 inch (22 cm) springform pan greased and lined with parchment (baking paper) and bake in a moderate oven (350°F/180°C/Gas Mark 4) for 50 minutes, or until a wooden skewer inserted in the middle comes out clean.

About 10 minutes before the cake is cooked, put the syrup ingredients into a saucepan over a medium heat and bring to simmering point. Reduce heat to low and simmer for 10 minutes. Strain the liquid into a jug and while it is still hot pour it very slowly over the hot cake. Cool the cake in the pan. Decorate with Toffee Bark and cream.

Serves 8

Buttermilk Cream with Rhubarb Coulis

¾ cup (6 oz/180 g) sugar
½ cup (4 fl oz/125 ml) water
5 teaspoons gelatin
¼ cup (2 fl oz/60 ml) water, extra

1½ cups (12 fl oz/375 ml)
buttermilk
1 cup (8 fl oz/250 ml) cream
1 tablespoon vanilla extract (essence)
Rhubarb Coulis, for serving

PUT THE sugar in a saucepan with ½ cup (4 fl oz/120 ml) water and bring to the boil, stirring until the sugar has dissolved. Remove from the heat.

Soften the gelatin in the extra water and stir over hot water to dissolve. Stir the dissolved gelatin into the sugar syrup then combine with the buttermilk. Put into the refrigerator until just starting to thicken.

Whip the cream until soft peaks form, add the vanilla extract, then fold into the buttermilk mixture. Pour into individual decorative bowls, cover with plastic (cling) wrap and refrigerate until set.

Spoon some Rhubarb Coulis onto each plate and serve the Buttermilk Cream on top.

Serves 6–8

RHUBARB COULIS

•

1 bunch rhubarb,
trimmed and chopped into
short pieces
¾ cup (6 oz/180 g) sugar
1 cup (8 fl oz/250 ml)
water

•

Put the rhubarb into a saucepan, then add the sugar and water. Cook uncovered, stirring occasionally, for about 10 minutes or until the rhubarb softens. Do not overcook or the rhubarb will lose its lovely pink tone. Purée in a food processor or blender.

•

Caramel Cream Pie

3 oz (90 g) butter, softened
¼ cup (2 oz/ 60 g) sugar
1 teaspoon vanilla extract (essence)
1 egg
3 oz (90 g) self-rising (raising) flour
3 oz (90 g) all-purpose (plain) flour
CARAMEL FILLING
4 oz (125 g) butter

1 cup (8 oz/250 g) packed (soft)
  brown sugar
¾ cup (6 fl oz/180 ml) light (single)
  cream
3 egg yolks
1 cup (8 fl oz/250 g) thick (double)
  cream, for serving
Toffee Bark, for serving

TO MAKE the pastry, cream the butter and sugar. Add the vanilla extract and egg and stir to combine. Sift the flour and stir into the mixture. Turn out onto a floured work surface and knead lightly. Wrap in plastic (cling) wrap and refrigerate for about 1 hour.

Grease an 8 inch (20 cm) pie plate.

Roll out the pastry on a floured work surface to fit the pie plate. Prick the base with a fork and pinch the edges to decorate. Bake in a hot oven (400°F/200°C/Gas Mark 6) for 15 minutes, then reduce the heat to moderate (350°F/180°C/Gas Mark 4) for another 5 minutes, or until pale golden brown. Set aside to cool.

To make the filling, melt the butter in a heavy saucepan and stir in the sugar until dissolved. Boil for 3 minutes. Remove from the heat, leave for a minute, then stir in the cream and then the egg yolks. Return to a very low heat and whisk continuously until thickened. Set aside to cool.

Pour the caramel filling into the pastry crust and top with a thick layer of whipped cream. Decorate with Toffee Bark.

Serves 6–8

TOFFEE BARK

•

oil
brown sugar
superfine (caster) sugar

Cover the broiler (griller) tray with a layer of foil. Brush with oil. Turn up the edges of the foil slightly to prevent spillage.

Sprinkle patches of the foil with a light covering of brown sugar and then with a light covering of superfine sugar. The bark will only form where the sugar completely covers the foil.

Put under a hot broiler. Remove the tray from the heat once the sugar melts or the sugar will burn. Leave to cool, then peel away the foil.

•

Cherry Clafouti

1 lb (500 g) fresh cherries, pitted
2 oz (60 g) all-purpose (plain) flour
½ teaspoon double-acting baking
   powder (1 teaspoon baking
   powder)
4 eggs

¾ cup (6 fl oz/180 ml) milk
½ cup (4 oz/125 g) sugar
2 oz (60 g) butter, melted
confectioners' (icing) sugar, for
   serving
Cherry Sauce, for serving

FRESH cherries make all the difference to this Clafouti. If not available substitute lightly poached sliced peaches, nectarines or apricots.

Put the cherries into an oven dish.

Place the remaining ingredients, except the confectioners' sugar, into a food processor or blender and process to combine. Or alternatively beat together until well combined.

Pour the batter over the cherries and bake in a moderately hot oven (400°F/200°C/Gas Mark 6) for about 40 minutes until puffed and golden. Sprinkle some confectioners' sugar over the top and serve immediately with Cherry Sauce.

Serves 6–8

CHERRY SAUCE

•

4 oz (125 g) sugar
½ cup (4 fl oz/125 ml)
   water
8 oz (250 g) fresh
   cherries, pitted
1 teaspoon cornstarch
   (cornflour)

•

Put the sugar and water into a saucepan and bring to simmering point, stirring to dissolve the sugar. Add the cherries and cook until tender but keeping their shape, about 5 minutes. Stir a tablespoon of the hot liquid into the cornstarch and when smooth pour into the simmering cherries. Stir until thickened then remove from the heat.

•

Chocolate Almond Cake

9 egg whites

pinch salt

6 oz (180 g) superfine (caster) sugar

10 oz (300 g) almonds, finely chopped

12 oz (375 g) semi-sweet (dark) chocolate, finely chopped

12 oz (375 g) seedless raisins

CHOCOLATE ICING

¼ cup (2 fl oz/60 ml) cream

4 oz (125 g) semi-sweet (dark) chocolate

1 oz (30 g) butter

Crystallized Rose Petals, for serving

GREASE and line a 12 inch (30 cm) springform pan with parchment (baking paper).

Beat the egg whites and the salt until soft peaks form. Gradually add the sugar, beating well after each addition until the mixture is thick and glossy. Gently fold in the almonds, then the chocolate and raisins.

Pour the mixture into the prepared pan and bake in a slow oven (320°F/170°C/Gas Mark 3) for about 1½ hours, or until a wooden skewer inserted in the middle comes out clean. Cool in the pan.

To make the icing, put the cream in a saucepan and bring to boiling point. Remove from the heat and stir in the chocolate until it melts, then stir in the butter. Set aside to cool, but do not allow the mixture to harden before spreading over the cake. Decorate with Crystallized Rose Petals.

Serves 15

CRYSTALLIZED ROSE PETALS

•

1 egg white

confectioners' (icing) sugar, sifted

red or pink roses

•

Line a tray with parchment (baking paper). Whip the egg white until frothy, but not stiff. Dip the rose petals or whole rose into the egg white. Allow any excess to drip away, then dip into the sugar. Shake to remove any excess. Place on the tray to dry overnight.

•

Chocolate Date Cake

4 oz (125 g) chocolate, roughly
    chopped
4 oz (125 g) blanched almonds,
    ground
3 oz (90 g) seeded dates, chopped

4 egg whites
pinch cream of tartar
¾ cup (6 oz/180 g) sugar
Chocolate Truffle Sauce (page 35),
    for serving

MELT the chocolate in a bowl over hot water. Set aside to cool (but not harden). Combine the almonds in a bowl with the dates.

Whip the egg whites with the cream of tartar until soft peaks form, then add the sugar gradually, beating continuously until thick and glossy. Fold through the almonds and dates, then fold through the melted chocolate.

Scrape into a 9 inch (22 cm) springform pan, greased and lined with parchment (baking paper), and cook in a moderate oven (350°F/180°C/Gas Mark 4) for about 50 minutes, or until a wooden skewer inserted in the middle comes out clean. Cool in the pan.

To serve, remove the sides of the pan and serve with Chocolate Truffle Sauce or lashings of whipped cream, strawberries and chocolate curls.

Serves 8

Chocolate Hazelnut Pavlova

6 egg whites
pinch salt
2 cups (16 oz/500 g) superfine
   (caster) sugar
2 teaspoons instant coffee powder
4 teaspoons cornstarch (cornflour)

2 teaspoons vinegar
hazelnuts, toasted and roughly
   chopped, to decorate
heavy (double) cream, whipped
Chocolate Truffle Sauce, for serving

IF YOU have a gas oven preheat it to a very hot (450°F/230°C/Gas Mark 8). If you have an electric oven preheat it to 300°F (150°C).

Beat the egg whites with salt until soft peaks form. Add the sugar a little at a time while continuing to beat. When all the sugar has been incorporated gently fold in the coffee powder, cornstarch and vinegar. Pile the mixture into a greased 8 inch (20 cm) springform pan.

If using a gas oven turn the heat to the lowest temperature, put in the pavlova and bake for 1½ hours, or until it crisps and browns a little on top.

If using an electric oven, put in the pavlova and cook for 45 minutes then turn off the oven and leave with the door shut for 1 hour.

When the pavlova is cooked remove from the oven and cool. Remove the side of the springform pan and fill the pavlova with cream. Pour the Chocolate Truffle Sauce over the cream and decorate with hazelnuts.

Serves 6–8

CHOCOLATE TRUFFLE
SAUCE

•

8 oz (250 g) semi-sweet
(dark) chocolate, chopped
¾ cup (6 fl oz/180 ml)
light (single) cream
3 oz (90 g) unsalted
butter
2 tablespoons rum
1¼ cups (10 fl oz/300 ml)
heavy (double) cream

•

Melt the chocolate in a
bowl over hot water.
Bring the light cream to
boiling point then
remove from the stove
and stir in the butter.
Stir the cream and butter
into the melted
chocolate until smooth.
Stir in the rum and
heavy cream.

•

Chocolate Pears

3 cups (24 fl oz/750 ml) water
½ cup (4 oz/125 g) sugar
1 tablespoon vanilla extract (essence)
4 pears with stalks intact, peeled

chocolate topping — a good store-
    bought brand will give a good
    result
Chocolate Leaves, for serving

PUT THE water, sugar and vanilla extract into a saucepan and bring to a simmering point.

Cut a thin slice from the base of each pear and stand them in the saucepan. Cook, covered, at simmering point for 10 minutes, or until the pears are tender but keeping their shape.

Lift the pears out of the liquid and stand them in a shallow bowl. Discard the liquid.

While the pears are still hot, pour enough chocolate topping over each pear to cover the surface. Set aside to cool.

Just before serving, decorate with Chocolate Leaves.

Serves 6

CHOCOLATE LEAVES

•

*8 citrus leaves
4 oz (125 g) chocolate*

•

Carefully wash and dry the leaves. Melt the chocolate in a bowl over hot water. Use a medium-sized paintbrush to thickly coat the underside of each leaf, taking care not to paint over the edges or the leaves will be impossible to separate. Put the leaves on a baking sheet and refrigerate until the chocolate hardens. When ready to use, peel the leaves away from the chocolate.

•

Chocolate Sauce Pudding

4 oz (125 g) butter, softened
4 oz (125 g) sugar
2 eggs
1 teaspoon vanilla extract (essence)
3 oz (90 g) self-rising (raising) flour,
1 oz (30 g) cocoa powder
½ teaspoon double-acting baking
   powder (1 teaspoon baking
   powder)

1 tablespoon milk
4 oz (125 g) packed (soft) brown
   sugar
1 oz (30 g) cocoa powder, extra
1¼ cups (10 fl oz/300 ml) hot
   water
thick (heavy) cream, for serving

CREAM the butter and sugar until light and fluffy. Add the eggs and extract and beat until creamy. Sift together the flour, cocoa powder and baking powder. Add to the butter and sugar mixture and beat well until combined. Stir in the milk. Scrape the mixture into a greased oven dish (40 fl oz/1.2 litre capacity).

Put the brown sugar and extra cocoa powder into a bowl and gradually stir in the hot water. Pour carefully over the pudding mixture.

Bake in a moderately hot oven (375°F/190°C/Gas Mark 5) for about 40 minutes, until firm to touch. Serve hot with cream.

Serves 4

Chocolate Truffles in Grand Marnier Icecream

¾ cup (6 oz/180 g) sugar

¼ cup (2 fl oz/60 ml) water

7 egg yolks

1 cup (8 fl oz/250 ml) heavy (double) cream

¼ cup (2 fl oz/60 ml) Grand Marnier

6 Chocolate Truffles

CHOCOLATE truffles are concealed in individual serves of superb Grand Marnier icecream. Both recipes are also excellent on their own.

To make the icecream, cook the sugar and water in a small heavy-based saucepan without stirring until the syrup reaches the soft ball stage (a little dropped in cold water forms a soft ball or 238°F/115°C on a candy thermometer).

Put the egg yolks in a food processor or blender and process while adding the hot sugar syrup in a thin stream. When all the syrup has been added, stop the machine but leave the mixture in it to cool. When cool, process again for about 1 minute.

In a separate bowl, lightly beat the thickened cream, then fold in the egg yolk and syrup mixture and the Grand Marnier.

Divide the mixture between six glass dishes, drop a Chocolate Truffle into each dish and freeze until firm.

Serves 6

CHOCOLATE TRUFFLES

•

3 oz (90 g) semi-sweet (dark) chocolate, roughly chopped

¼ cup (2 fl oz/60 ml) light (single) cream

1 oz (30 g) butter

1 tablespoon Grand Marnier

•

Melt the chocolate in a bowl over hot water. Bring the cream to boiling point then remove from the stove and stir in the butter. Stir the cream and butter into the melted chocolate until smooth. Stir in the Grand Marnier. Refrigerate until firm, then shape the mixture into six rough balls.

•

Cointreau Icecream

4 eggs, separated
1 cup (5 oz/150 g) confectioners'
   (icing) sugar
1¼ cups (10 fl oz/300 ml)
   thickened cream
½ cup (4 fl oz/125 ml) condensed
   milk

¼ cup (2 fl oz/60 ml) Cointreau
TOPPING
1½ cups (12 fl oz/375 ml) orange
   juice
¼ cup (2 fl oz/60 ml) Cointreau

TO MAKE the icecream, line a 4 x 8 inch (10 x 20 cm) loaf pan or 9 inch (22 cm) round springform pan with greased foil.

Beat the egg whites until soft peaks form then gradually beat in the sugar. Lightly beat the egg yolks and fold into the egg white mixture. Whip the cream until soft peaks form then gradually beat in the condensed milk. Fold the cream and condensed milk into the egg mixture then stir in the Cointreau.

Pour evenly into the pan and freeze until firm.

To make the topping, pour the orange juice into a saucepan and simmer to reduce to about 1 cup (8 fl oz/250 ml). Cool, then add the Cointreau and pour carefully over the firm icecream.

Freeze, then cover with plastic (cling) wrap.

To serve remove the icecream from the pan, transfer to a plate and cut into slices or wedges.

Serves 8

Cold Rum and Coconut Soufflé

1 cup (8 fl oz/250 ml) coconut
    cream
3 teaspoons cornstarch (cornflour)
2 teaspoons gelatin
¼ cup (2 fl oz/60 ml) water
4 eggs, separated

few drops vanilla extract (essence)
4 oz (125 g) superfine (caster) sugar
4 oz (125 g) plain cake crumbs
½ cup (3 fl oz/90 ml) white rum
pinch salt

PUT THE coconut cream in a saucepan and heat gently. Dissolve the cornstarch in a small amount of water and add to the saucepan. Stir with a wooden spoon until the mixture reaches simmering point and starts to thicken. Set aside.

Sprinkle the gelatin in the water and stir over hot water to dissolve.

Beat the egg yolks, vanilla extract and sugar until pale and thick then add, with the dissolved gelatin, to the coconut cream. Cook gently over a very low heat, stirring constantly with a wooden spoon for 5 minutes. Stir in the cake crumbs and the white rum and take off the heat.

Beat the egg whites with the pinch of salt until soft peaks form, then fold them into the coconut mixture while it is still warm but not hot.

Pour into a fluted pan and refrigerate until firm. Turn out and decorate.

Serves 6

Crepes with Zabaglione Sauce

1 cup (5 oz/150 g) all-purpose
   (plain) flour
pinch salt
1 egg, lightly beaten
1¼ cups (10 fl oz/300 ml) skim
   milk or use half milk, half water

1 teaspoon vanilla extract (essence)
1 oz (30 g) butter
fresh fruit, for serving
Zabaglione Sauce, for serving

PUT the crepe ingredients, except the butter, in a food processor or blender and blend for only a few seconds until just combined. Or alternatively, whisk lightly in a bowl. Do not overmix or the crepes will be tough — it doesn't matter if there are a few small lumps. The mixture should be the consistency of thin cream — if too thick add a little more skim milk.

Transfer the batter to a jug.

Melt a teaspoon of butter in an omelet pan over medium heat and pour in just enough batter to thinly cover the base of the pan — you may have to tilt the pan to make the batter spread quickly.

When the underside is pale brown, turn over and lightly brown the other side. Transfer to a plate, cover with foil and keep warm in a low oven. Repeat the process to cook the rest of the batter. Give the batter an occasional light stir if it starts to settle.

When ready to serve, take the crepes out of the oven, fold each one in quarters and place on warmed individual dishes. Decorate with fresh sliced fruit or berries. Pour over the Zabaglione Sauce.

Makes 8–10 depending on the size of the pan

ZABAGLIONE SAUCE

•

4 egg yolks
4 tablespoons superfine
(caster) sugar
4 tablespoons champagne

•

To make the sauce put all of the ingredients in the top of a double boiler or in a heatproof bowl placed over a pan of hot water. Whisk over water that is kept just below boiling point until fluffy, light and thickened (about 20–25 minutes). Chill until required.

•

Duo of Fruit Sauces with Almond Tuiles

MANGO COULIS

3 mangoes
2 oz (60 g) confectioners' (icing)
　sugar
juice of 1 lime
¼ cup (2 fl oz/60 ml) white rum

RASPBERRY SAUCE

1 lb (500 g) frozen raspberries
1 oz (30 g) confectioners' (icing)
　sugar
Cassis (blackcurrant liqueur),
　optional
icecream, for serving
Almond Tuiles, for serving

TO MAKE the Mango Coulis, peel the mangoes and use a sharp serrated knife to cut as much flesh off the seeds as possible — do this on a plate to save the juice. Put the mangoes and juice into a food processor or blender with the remaining ingredients and purée. Keep in a covered container in the refrigerator until ready to use. This recipe freezes satisfactorily.

To make the Raspberry Sauce, defrost or partially defrost the raspberries. Transfer to a food processor or blender, add the sugar and process until smooth. Refrigerate until ready to use. This recipe also keeps well in the freezer. A few tablespoons of Cassis (blackcurrant liqueur) makes a delicious addition to this sauce.

Serve with icecream and Almond Tuiles.

Serves 6–8

ALMOND TUILES

•

2 egg whites
½ cup (4 oz/125 g)
superfine (caster) sugar
3 oz (90 g) all-purpose
(plain) flour, sifted
1 teaspoon vanilla extract
(essence)
1 oz (30 g) flaked almonds
2 oz (60 g) butter, melted

•

Beat the egg whites until soft peaks form, then gradually beat in the sugar. Fold in the remaining ingredients. Drop spoonfuls onto greased baking sheets, leaving room for spreading. Bake at 375°F (190°C/Gas Mark 5) for 8 minutes, or until golden. Drape over a rolling pin until cool.

•

Flourless Orange Almond Cake

2 oranges
6 oz (180 g) blanched almonds
6 eggs
pinch salt
8 oz (250 g) sugar

½ teaspoon double-acting baking
    powder (1 teaspoon baking
    powder)
2 teaspoons vanilla extract (essence)
apricot jam, for serving

PUT THE oranges in a saucepan and add enough hot water to cover. Bring to the boil and simmer for about 30 minutes or until very soft.

Meanwhile, grease and line a 10 inch (25 cm) springform pan.

Drain and cool the oranges then cut into quarters and remove the seeds.

Process the almonds in a food processor or blender — do this gradually so that some of the nuts are ground fine, others coarse. Tip the almonds into a bowl and set aside. Put the eggs into the food processor and pulse until lightly beaten. Tip into a bowl and set aside. Put the oranges into the food processor and blend until smooth. Add the salt, sugar, baking powder and vanilla extract and process until just combined. Add the almonds and process until just combined. Add the eggs and process until just blended.

Pour the mixture into the prepared pan and bake in a moderate oven (375°F/190°C/Gas Mark 5) for about 50 minutes, until golden brown and firm to the touch. Cool in the pan. Heat some apricot jam and brush over the surface of the cake before serving.

Serves 8–10

Fruit and Nut Meringue

6 egg whites
15 oz (475 g) sugar
6 oz (180 g) stoned dates, coarsely
    chopped
4 oz (125 g) pecans, coarsely
    chopped

4 oz (125 g) semi-sweet (dark)
    chocolate, coarsely chopped
2 oz (60 g) crystallized ginger, finely
    chopped
heavy (double) cream, for serving
fresh fruit, for serving

BEAT THE egg whites until stiff peaks form, then gradually beat in the sugar. Fold in the remaining ingredients.

Pour 3 inch (7 cm) circles of the mixture onto a baking sheet covered with greased parchment (baking paper) and bake in a moderately slow oven (325°F/170°C/Gas Mark 3) for 40–50 minutes or until a wooden skewer inserted in the middle comes out clean.

Cool on the baking sheet. If desired the meringues can be frozen at this stage.

To serve, make small stacks of meringues by joining three together with whipped cream. Decorate with fresh fruit.

Serves 4–6

Hazelnut Bavarian

3 teaspoons gelatin
6 teaspoons cold water
½ cup (4 fl oz/125 ml) milk
¼ cup (2 oz/60 g) sugar
4 egg yolks
4 oz (125 g) ground hazelnuts

1 teaspoon vanilla extract (essence)
1 cup (8 fl oz/250 ml) heavy
   (double) cream
cocoa powder, for serving
Caramel Sauce (page 19), for serving

SOAK the gelatin in the water and stir over hot water to dissolve.

Scald the milk. In the top of a double saucepan over boiling water, beat the sugar and egg yolks. Start adding the hot milk gradually, stirring continuously until the mixture starts to thicken. Stir in the dissolved gelatin then the ground hazelnuts and the vanilla extract. Refrigerate until just starting to set.

Whip the cream until soft peaks form and fold into the mixture. Pour into a serving dish or individual decorative molds and return to the refrigerator until ready to serve. Sprinkle with cocoa powder and serve with Caramel Sauce if desired.

Serves 4

Hazelnut Waffles with Caramel Sauce

4 oz (125 g) all-purpose (plain)
 flour, sifted
½ teaspoon double-acting baking
 powder (1 teaspoon baking
 powder)
4 oz (125 g) hazelnuts, finely
 ground
2 tablespoons sugar

1¼ cups (10 fl oz/300 ml)
 buttermilk
1 egg, lightly beaten
1 teaspoon vanilla extract (essence)
1 oz (30 g) butter, melted
icecream, for serving
Caramel Sauce (page 19), for serving

THESE waffles are a delectable dessert. Also try them with poached fruit
and thick cream or yogurt; they are wonderful with caramel icecream and
maple syrup, or vanilla icecream with caramel sauce or a fruit purée. For a
dinner party make ahead and freeze; to serve, simply warm for a few
minutes in a moderate oven.

Combine the flour, baking powder and hazelnuts in a bowl. Make a
well in the middle, add the sugar, buttermilk, egg and extract and mix to a
smooth batter.

Brush a waffle iron with melted butter and heat. Pour in 2 to 3
tablespoons of the mixture, taking care that it does not overflow. Close the
iron and cook for 3–4 minutes until the waffle is golden brown and crisp.
Repeat with the remaining mixture.

Serve with icecream and Caramel Sauce.

Makes 6

Individual Raspberry Soufflés with Apricot Purée

butter and superfine (caster) sugar,
    for preparing the soufflé dishes
12 oz (375 g) raspberries (frozen or
    fresh)
5 oz (150 g) confectioners' (icing)
    sugar

juice of ½ lemon
4 egg yolks
12 egg whites
pinch salt
Apricot Purée, for serving

GREASE six individual (4 inch/10 cm) soufflé dishes with butter, then sprinkle lightly with sugar.

Put the raspberries into a food processor or blender (defrosting first if necessary) then add 3 oz (90 g) of the confectioners' sugar and the lemon juice. Purée.

Add the egg yolks and process briefly, then transfer to a large bowl.

Put the egg whites and the salt into another large bowl (preferably stainless steel or copper) and beat until soft peaks form (do not make them too stiff). Gradually add the rest of the sugar while continuing to beat. Using a spoon stir about one-third of the egg whites into the raspberry purée then, using a spatula, lightly fold in the remainder.

Fill the soufflé dishes with the mixture and cook in a hot oven (425°F/ 220°C/Gas Mark 7) for about 12 minutes. Serve immediately with Apricot Purée if desired.

Serves 6

APRICOT PUREE

•

8 oz (250 g) dried apricots
1 cup (8 fl oz/250 ml)
    water
½ cup (4 oz/125 g) sugar
¼ cup (2 fl oz/60 ml)
Amaretto (almond liqueur)

•

Put the apricots and water into a saucepan and leave to soak for about 1 hour. Add the sugar and a little more water if necessary (the fruit should not be quite covered) and bring to simmering point. Stir and cook for about 15 minutes. Transfer to a food processor or blender, add the Amaretto and purée.

•

Lemon Sauterne Cream

6 eggs, separated
grated peel (rind) and juice
    of 1 lemon
5 oz (150 g) sugar

2 teaspoons gelatin
¼ cup (2 fl oz/60 ml) water
1 cup (8 fl oz/250 ml) sauterne

PUT THE egg yolks into a food processor or blender and start processing.

Add the lemon peel and juice and the sugar and continue processing for a few minutes until light and creamy.

Soften the gelatin in the water and stir to dissolve over hot water.

Place the sauterne in a saucepan and bring to simmering point then remove from the heat. Add the gelatin to the sauterne and stir.

Turn on the food processor again and gradually add the sauterne and gelatin to the egg yolk mixture. Transfer to a bowl.

Beat the egg whites until soft peaks form then fold gently into the mixture.

Pour into six glass serving dishes and chill.

Serves 6

Lime Pie

3 oz (90 g) butter

3 oz (90 g) sugar

1 egg

3 oz (90 g) self-rising (raising)
  flour, sifted

3 oz (90 g) all-purpose (plain) flour,
  sifted

LIME FILLING

1 cup (10 fl oz/300 ml) lime juice

finely grated peel (rind) of 4 limes

½ cup (4 oz/125 g) sugar

1 oz (30 g) butter

1 oz (30 g) all-purpose (plain) flour

3 egg yolks

MERINGUE

3 egg whites

pinch of cream of tartar

½ cup (4 oz/125 g) sugar

CREAM the butter and sugar, then stir in the egg. Add the flours to the mixture
and stir well. Knead the dough lightly, wrap in plastic (cling) wrap and refrigerate
for 1 hour. Roll out the pastry to fit a greased 8 inch (20 cm) pie plate. Prick the
base with a fork. Bake in a hot oven (400°F/200°C/Gas Mark 6) for 15 minutes,
then reduce the temperature to moderate (350°F/180°C/Gas Mark 4) and bake
for another 5 minutes or until the pastry is golden. Set aside to cool.

In a saucepan warm the lime juice, peel and sugar, stirring to dissolve the
sugar. Melt the butter in separate heavy saucepan. Stir in the flour to make a
smooth paste. Gradually stir in the lime juice mixture. When it starts to simmer,
remove from the heat and stir in the egg yolks, one at a time. Return to a low heat
and stir until the mixture thickens. Set aside to cool.

Pour the lime filling into the pastry crust. To make the meringue, beat the egg
whites and the cream of tartar until soft peaks form. Gradually beat in the sugar
until thick and glossy. Pipe on to the pie and bake in a moderate oven (350°F/
180°C/Gas Mark 4) for 15 minutes, or until the meringue is golden.

Serves 6–8

Macadamia and Pecan Tart

6 oz (180 g) plain sweet crackers
1 cup (3 oz/90 g) unsweetened
   (desiccated) coconut
4 oz (125 g) butter, melted
FILLING
4 oz (125 g) unsalted macadamia
   nuts

2 oz (60 g) pecan nuts
3 eggs, beaten
¾ cup (6 fl oz/180 ml) maple syrup
½ cup (4 fl oz/125 ml) honey
3 oz (90 g) butter, melted
heavy (double) cream, for serving

TO MAKE the crust, process the crackers and coconut in a food processor or blender until finely ground. Transfer to a bowl and stir in the melted butter until combined. Press into a greased 10 inch (25 cm) pie dish and refrigerate until firm.

To make the filling, place the macadamia and pecan nuts evenly over the surface of the prepared crust. Beat the remaining ingredients together and pour over the nuts.

Cook in a slow oven (325°F/170°C/Gas Mark 3) for about 45 minutes, until golden brown and firm on top.

Serve warm, or at room temperature with cream.

Serves 8

Mascarpone with Amaretto

8 oz (250 g) mascarpone
¼ cup (1 oz/30 g) confectioners'
    (icing) sugar
½ cup (4 fl oz/125 ml) Amaretto
    (almond liqueur)

fruit in season — apricots, figs,
    grapes, peaches, strawberries,
    raspberries are all suitable
cookies, store bought Italian-style

PUT THE mascarpone and sugar into a bowl and mix well.

Make a shallow well in the middle and pour in the Amaretto — stir through.

Serve with fresh fruit and Italian style cookies such as Almond Bread. Other serving ideas:

• Mascapone with Amaretto Biscotti dipped in strong black coffee.

• Individual pastry cases made from shortcrust pastry filled with mascapone and decorated with glacé orange peel (rind).

• Mascapone with glacé pineapple, cherries, apricots and pears.

• Mascapone made with Galliano instead of Amaretto and served with a fresh fruit purée.

Serves 6

Meringue Supreme

4 oz (125 g) Individual Meringues
   (page 103)
½ cup (4 fl oz/125 ml) Raspberry
   Sauce (page 49)

1 punnet (8 oz/250 g) strawberries,
   hulled
1 cup (8 fl oz/250 ml) heavy
   (double) cream

CUT THE meringues into quarters. Halve the strawberries and toss in Raspberry Sauce. Place the meringues in a bowl. Add the Raspberry Sauce and the strawberries to the meringues and mix together gently.

Whip the cream until soft peaks form and fold lightly through the meringue and fruit mixture — the cream and Rasberry Sauce should not be too thoroughly mixed together. Pile the mixture into four glass serving dishes and chill.

Serves 4

Orange Rice with Spiced Oranges

1½ cups (12 fl oz/375 ml) orange
    juice
juice of 1 lemon
1½ oz (45 g) butter
½ cup (4 oz/125 g) packed (soft)
    brown sugar

10 oz (300 g) short-grain rice
1¼ cups (10 fl oz/300 ml) cream
4 teaspoons grated orange peel (rind)
4 tablespoons Grand Marnier

PUT THE fruit juices, butter and sugar into a heavy-based saucepan and stir over low heat until the sugar dissolves. Add the rice, stir well, and continue cooking over low heat, stirring every few minutes, until almost all the liquid is absorbed — about 15 minutes.

Add the cream, stir well and continue cooking over low heat, stirring constantly, until almost all the cream is absorbed — about 5–10 minutes. Check that the rice is cooked through — if further cooking is necessary add a little more cream or some milk. Use a fork to mix through the orange peel and Grand Marnier. Serve hot or cold with Spiced Oranges and cream or icecream.

Serves 6

SPICED ORANGES

•

3 large oranges, cut into
thick slices

water

1 cup (8 oz/250 g) sugar

1 cup (8 fl oz/250 ml)
honey

1 cinnamon stick

•

Simmer the orange slices in enough water to cover for 20 minutes or until tender. Drain and set aside. Combine the remaining ingredients in a saucepan and bring to the boil. Add the orange slices and simmer over a low heat for 20 minutes or until coated with syrup. Remove the cinnamon stick.

•

Panettone Custard with Whiskey Sauce

2 oz (60 g) golden raisins (sultanas)
¼ cup (2 fl oz/60 ml) sherry
6 slices Panettone
softened butter
apricot jam
3 eggs

4 tablespoons superfine (caster) sugar
2 cups (16 fl oz/500 ml) light
  (single) cream
1 teaspoon vanilla extract (essence)
Whiskey Sauce, for serving

SOAK the raisins in the sherry for about 30 minutes. Cut the Panettone into slices about ½ inch/1¼ cm thick. Butter the slices and spread with apricot jam. Butter an oven dish 6–7 cup (48 fl oz/1½ litre) capacity and put the slices of Panettone into the dish in one layer. Sprinkle the raisins over the bread.

Beat the eggs and sugar then add the milk, cream and vanilla extract and continue beating until just combined. Pour through a sieve over the bread, taking care to moisten all the slices.

Stand the dish in a baking pan and pour boiling water into the baking pan to come about halfway up the side of the dish containing the custard. Bake in a slow oven (325°F/170°C/Gas Mark 3) for about 50 minutes until set and golden brown on top. Serve warm with Whiskey Sauce.

Serves 6–8

WHISKEY SAUCE

•

½ cup (4 fl oz/125 ml)
  honey
½ cup (4 fl oz/125 ml)
  whiskey
1 oz (30 g) butter, cut into
  small pieces

•

Put the honey and whiskey into a small saucepan and bring slowly to simmering point. Add the butter gradually, stirring to combine.

•

Panforte with Chantilly Cream

3 oz (90 g) hazelnuts
3 oz (90 g) coarsely chopped
    blanched almonds
3 oz (90 g) candied peel (rind),
    finely chopped
1½ oz (45 g) cocoa
2½ oz (75 g) all-purpose (plain)
    flour, sifted

½ teaspoon ground cinnamon
½ teaspoon ground nutmeg
½ cup (4 oz/125 g) sugar
⅓ cup (3 fl oz/90 ml) honey
confectioners' (icing) sugar, for
    serving
Chantilly Cream, for serving

COMBINE all of the ingredients except the sugar, honey and confectioners' sugar in a bowl.

Put the sugar and honey in a saucepan and heat slowly, stirring, until the sugar dissolves. Bring to boiling point and continue cooking until a little of the mixture dropped into cold water forms a soft ball, or a candy thermometer reaches 240°F (115°C). Add the syrup to the other ingredients and stir to combine.

Transfer the mixture to an 8 inch (20 cm) greased pan lined with parchment (baking paper). Use a spatula to smooth and flatten the surface.

Bake in a slow oven (300°F/150°C/Gas Mark 2) for 35 minutes. Cool in the pan, then turn out and sprinkle liberally with confectioners' sugar and cinnamon. Cut into slices to serve. You can serve it on its own or as a dessert with a dollop of Chantilly Cream.

Serves 10–12

CHANTILLY CREAM

•

1¼ cups (10 fl oz/300 ml)
    cream
1 heaped tablespoon
confectioners' (icing) sugar
1 teaspoon vanilla extract
    (essence)

•

Whip the cream until soft peaks form then add the confectioners' sugar and vanilla extract.
VARIATION: Add 1–2 teaspoons of instant coffee powder.

•

Passionfruit Soufflé

butter and superfine (caster) sugar,
*   for preparing the soufflé dishes*
20 passionfruit

3 egg yolks
6 oz (180 g) sugar
6 egg whites

GREASE an 8 inch (20 cm) soufflé dish with butter, then sprinkle lightly with superfine sugar. Scrape the pulp from 5 passionfruit into a small bowl.

Beat the egg yolks with half the sugar until the mixture becomes pale and frothy, then stir in the passionfruit pulp.

In a separate bowl (preferably stainless steel or copper) beat the egg whites until soft peaks form (do not make them too stiff), then gradually add the remaining sugar while continuing to beat.

Using a spoon, stir about one-third of the egg white into the egg yolk and passionfruit mixture then, using a spatula, lightly fold in the remainder.

Fill the soufflé dish with the mixture and cook in a hot oven (425°F/220°C/Gas Mark 7) for 15–20 minutes, until the soufflé is puffed and golden brown.

While the soufflé cooks (or this can be done in advance) scrape the pulp from the remaining 15 passionfruit into a small saucepan and warm gently with a small amount of sugar to taste. Transfer the juice to a sauceboat.

Serve at the table as soon as the soufflé is cooked.

Serves 4

Pears in Pastry

2 oz (60 g) butter, softened
2 oz (60 g) soft brown sugar
4 oz (125 g) ground almonds
1 tablespoon Amaretto (almond
   liqueur)

6 pears
1 lb (500 g) ready rolled puff pastry
1 egg, beaten

CREAM the butter and sugar until light and fluffy, then stir in the ground almonds and Amaretto. Set aside.

Taking care to leave the stalk of each pear intact, remove the cores from the pears, digging carefully from the base. Parboil the pears, about 5 minutes — the pears should still be firm and holding their shape. Set aside until cool. Fill the pears with the ground almond mixture.

On a lightly floured surface, roll out the pastry until very thin. Cut the pastry into six squares about 9 inches (22 cm). Stand each pear in the middle of a pastry square then lift up the edges of the pastry to enclose the pear, leaving the stalk exposed. Pinch the edges of the pastry together to seal, then brush the pastry with the beaten egg. Use some of the pastry scraps to make decorative leaves: cut them out two at a time connected by a long stem, which can be twisted around each pear stalk. Chill the pastry-wrapped pears in the refrigerator for 1 hour or more (or prepare the day before and leave overnight).

Brush again with beaten egg. Bake in a hot oven (400°F/200°C/Gas Mark 6) for about 30 minutes, or until the pastry is golden brown. Serve hot with cream or icecream.

Serves 6

Pineapple and Avocado Ice with Crostoli

1½ cups (18 oz/560 g) crushed
    fresh pineapple
½ cup (4 oz/125 g) mashed avocado
¾ cup (6 oz/180 g) superfine
    (caster) sugar
4 teaspoons lemon juice
CROSTOLI
1 cup (5 oz/150 g) all-purpose
    (plain) flour, sifted

1 egg
1 teaspoon superfine (caster) sugar
1 teaspoon olive oil
sweet white wine, if required
olive oil for frying, extra
confectioners' (icing) sugar, for
    serving

PROCESS the pineapple, avocado, sugar and lemon juice in a food processor or blender. Transfer to a shallow container and put into the freezer.

After the mixture starts to freeze, stir occasionally with a fork to break up any larger crystals. For a smoother texture reprocess in the food processor or blender 1 hour before serving and return to the freezer.

To make the Crostoli, break the egg into the flour, add the sugar and oil and beat lightly with a fork. Mix the flour into the egg mixture and work into a smooth ball, adding a little wine to moisten if necessary. Chill for 30 minutes.

Roll out thinly. Using a pastry wheel cut the dough into strips about 3 inches (7 cm) wide and 6 inches (15 cm) long. Cut a 4 inch (9 cm) slit down the middle of each strip. Turn one end through the slit making a twist in the sides. Deep fry the strips in hot oil for about 4 minutes or until puffed and golden on both sides. When cold, sprinkle with sugar and serve.

Serves 6

Pineapple Delicious Pudding

1½ oz (45 g) butter, softened
½ cup (4 oz/125 g) sugar
1 oz (30 g) self-rising (raising) flour, sifted

4 oz (125 g) well-drained crushed pineapple
2 eggs, separated
¾ cup (6 fl oz/180 ml) milk
confectioners' (icing) sugar, to serve

THIS pudding is a cross between a cake and a custard. It is the ideal dessert when you want something warm but light.

Cream the butter and sugar, then add the flour and combine well. Mix in the crushed pineapple.

Whisk the egg yolks into the milk, then pour slowly into the mixture, beating constantly.

In a separate bowl, beat the egg whites until soft peaks form. Stir about one-quarter of the beaten egg whites into the mixture, then fold in the remainder.

Pour into a greased ovenproof dish and bake in a moderate oven (375°F/190°C/Gas Mark 5) for about 40 minutes until golden brown. The top should be a cakey crust which turns to a baked custard consistency underneath. Serve sprinkled with confectioners' sugar and with cream or icecream.

Serves 4

Plum Pudding

32 fl oz (1 litre) softened
    macadamia or vanilla icecream
plum pudding, sliced

Hard Sauce
Caramel Sauce (page 19), for
    serving

THIS recipe turns a bought plum pudding — or even Christmas pudding leftovers — into a luscious treat.

Put the icecream into the bottom of a large rounded bowl and smooth the surface — it should come about halfway up the sides.

Cover the icecream with thick slices of pudding, patting down firmly. Make sure that there are no gaps and that the surface is even and level with the top of the bowl. Cover with plastic (cling) wrap or foil and leave in the freezer until firmly set.

Turn the pudding out onto a flat plate (if necessary, dip briefly in warm water to loosen).

Spread the Hard Sauce over the icecream and the sides of the pudding, so that it is completely covered. Return to the freezer until the Hard Sauce is firm. Cover with plastic (cling) wrap or foil, pressed close to the surface, and leave in the freezer until ready to serve. To serve, pour over Caramel Sauce and cut in wedges like a cake.

HARD SAUCE

•

6 oz (180 g) butter
2 cups (9 oz/275 g)
confectioners' (icing) sugar
¼ cup (2 fl oz/60 ml)
brandy or rum

•

Put the butter into a bowl and beat until creamy, then continue beating while adding the sugar then the brandy or rum, until the mixture is light and fluffy.

•

Raspberry and Apricot Mousse

4 teaspoons gelatin
½ cup (4 fl oz/125 ml) water
8 oz (250 g) drained canned apricots
    or drained stewed apricots
¼ cup (2 fl oz/60 ml) apricot syrup
    (from the can or the liquid from
    the stewed apricots)

8 oz (250 g) raspberries
1 tablespoon confectioners' (icing)
    sugar
2 egg whites
1 tablespoon superfine (caster) sugar
½ cup (4 fl oz/125 ml) thickened
    cream

SOFTEN half the gelatin in half the water and stir over hot water to dissolve. Roughly purée the apricots in a food processor or blender. Transfer to a bowl and add the apricot syrup and dissolved gelatin and refrigerate until starting to set.

Soften the other half of the gelatin in the remaining water and stir over hot water to dissolve. Purée the raspberries with the confectioners' sugar in a food processor or blender. Transfer to another bowl, add the dissolved gelatin and refrigerate until starting to set.

Beat the egg whites until soft peaks form then add the superfine sugar gradually, beating until thick and glossy. Fold the egg whites into the apricot mixture. In another bowl, whip the cream until soft peaks form. Fold into the raspberry mixture.

Spoon raspberry mixture followed by apricot mixture into serving glasses — the different hues of the apricots and raspberries should remain distinct.

Serves 6

Raspberry Chocolate Cups

6 oz (180 g) semi-sweet (dark)
  chocolate, chopped
2 cups (16 fl oz/500 ml) heavy
  (double) cream
quarter of a vanilla bean
4 egg yolks

4 oz (125 g) sugar
1 cup (8 fl oz/250 ml) milk
2 tablespoons Kirsch
Raspberry Sauce (page 49), for
  serving

MELT the chocolate in a bowl over hot water. Put twelve paper patty cases
in a muffin pan. Divide the melted chocolate between the paper cases and
use the back of a teaspoon to spread the chocolate evenly over the sides
and base of the paper cases. Chill until the chocolate hardens.

Heat the cream and vanilla bean in a saucepan to simmering. Beat the
egg yolks, add half the sugar and beat well. Pour some of the hot cream
into the egg mixture, stirring constantly. Gradually add the remaining
cream, stirring all the time. Add the remaining sugar and stir gently over a
low heat until the custard thickens and coats the back of a spoon. Do not
allow it to boil.

Remove from the heat, add the milk and pour the custard into a bowl
to cool. Remove the vanilla bean. When cold stir in the Kirsch and freeze.
Stir the mixture 3 or 4 times during freezing to break down the ice crystals
or freeze in an icecream maker.

Peel the paper carefully off the chocolate cases. Place a scoop of
icecream into each case and serve with Raspberry Sauce.

Makes 12

Rum and Apple Brulée

1 oz (30 g) butter
2 oz (60 g) slivered almonds
12 oz (375 g) canned pie apples
2 oz (60 g) seedless raisins
2 tablespoons rum

1¼ cups (10 fl oz /300 ml)
  heavy (double) cream, whipped
3 tablespoons superfine (caster) sugar
2 tablespoons (soft) brown sugar

HERE is an easy version of the classic Creme Brulée — and just as delicious. Try it also with mixed berries or seedless grapes, which makes it even simpler because the fruit doesn't require cooking.

Melt the butter in a pan then sauté the almonds for 1–2 minutes until they start to brown. Add the apples and raisins and sauté for a few minutes, then stir through the rum and cook for about 1 minute. Divide the mixture between six individual dishes and leave to cool.

Spread the cream over the top of the fruit. Transfer to the freezer for about 30 minutes until almost, but not quite, frozen.

Combine the sugars and sprinkle evenly over the cream. Brown the sugar under the broiler (grill) — if you can't fit all the dishes under so they receive maximum heat do this in two stages.

Serves 6

Simply Luscious Icecreams

It's easy to transform store-bought icecream into a taste sensation.

• Add chopped preserved ginger and some of the syrup to softened vanilla icecream and refreeze.

• Add crushed macaroons and Grand Marnier to softened vanilla icecream and refreeze, or try crushed almond macaroons and Amaretto.

• Add chopped semi-sweet (dark) chocolate and Tia Maria to softened chocolate icecream and refreeze.

• Swirl Caramel Sauce (page 19) or butterscotch sauce and chopped hazelnuts through softened vanilla icecream and refreeze.

• Add fresh mango purée to softened vanilla icecream, stir well and refreeze.

• Add chopped glacé apricots and cherries, and raisins soaked in rum overnight to softened vanilla or chocolate icecream. Stir well and refreeze.

• Melt some dark chocolate in a bowl over hot water, cool, then swirl through softened chocolate ice-cream and refreeze.

• Stir Raspberry Sauce (page 49) through softened strawberry icecream and refreeze.

• Crush toffee-coated almonds and stir with honey through softened vanilla icecream and refreeze.

• Stir Apricot Purée (page 59) through softened vanilla icecream and refreeze.

NOTE: These additional ingredients can also be used as toppings for icecream.

Sticky Date Pudding

2 oz (60 g) butter, softened
6 oz (180 g) sugar
2 eggs
1 cup (8 fl oz/240 ml) water
6 oz (180 g) pitted dates
1 teaspoon baking soda (bicarbonate
  of soda)

6 oz (180 g) self-rising (raising)
  flour, sifted
heavy (double) cream, for serving
Caramel Sauce (page 19), for serving

CREAM the butter and sugar until light and fluffy. Add the eggs, one at a time, and continue beating until well combined.

Put the water and dates in a saucepan, bring to boil, add the baking soda, stir to dissolve, and remove from the heat.

Fold the flour into the butter, sugar and egg mixture, then fold in the date and water mixture.

Grease and flour an oven dish 6–7 cup (48 fl oz/1½ litre) capacity. Pour in mixture and spread evenly.

Bake in a moderately slow oven (325°F/170°C/Gas Mark 3), for 45 — 50 minutes or until wooden skewer inserted in the middle comes out clean. Turn the tray around once in the oven during cooking.

Serve warm with cream and if desired Caramel Sauce.

Serves 8

Strawberries Jellied in Red Wine

3 cups (26 fl oz/800 ml) red wine
1½ cups (12 oz/375 g) sugar
1 vanilla bean
2 strips orange peel (rind) from
    about ½ orange

1 cup (8 fl oz/250 ml) water
3 punnets (about 1½ lb/750 g)
    strawberries, hulled
gelatin

PUT ALL of the ingredients except the strawberries and gelatin into a saucepan, bring to the boil and simmer for 15 minutes. Leave to cool, preferably overnight — this allows any sediment in the wine to settle.

Remove the vanilla bean and orange peel from the syrup, and transfer the syrup back to a saucepan, taking care not to include any sediment.

Bring the syrup to simmering point and add some of the strawberries (about one punnet at a time) to the syrup. Bring back to simmering point and poach the strawberries for about 1 minute. Use a slotted spoon to transfer them to a plate to cool. Continue doing this until all the strawberries have been poached.

Measure the syrup carefully in a measuring jug — you should have about 3 cups (26 fl oz/750 ml). Measure 1½ teaspoons of gelatin for each cup (8 fl oz/240 ml) of syrup, soften in a small amount of cold water and stir to dissolve over hot water. Stir the dissolved gelatin into the syrup.

Arrange the berries decoratively in six glasses or bowls and pour some jelly into each one — the fruit should not be completely covered with jelly. Cover each one with plastic (cling) wrap and refrigerate to set.

Serves 6

Strawberry Layer Cake

4 eggs
4 oz (125g) superfine (caster) sugar
1 teaspoon vanilla extract (essence)
5 oz (150 g) all-purpose (plain)
    flour, sifted
2 oz (60 g) butter, melted and
    cooled

Chantilly Cream (page 75)
1 punnet (8 oz/250 g) strawberries,
    hulled and sliced
1 cup (4 fl oz/125 g) heavy (double)
    cream, whipped
extra whole strawberries for
    decoration

PUT THE eggs, sugar and vanilla in bowl, and place the bowl over a
saucepan of warm water. Place saucepan on a gentle heat.

Whisk until the mixture is thick and a lemon hue, and double in
volume — about 5–10 minutes. Remove the bowl from the heat and
continue whisking for about 4 minutes, or until cool and very thick. Fold
in the flour, then the butter, mixing as quickly and lightly as possible.
Immediately pour the mixture into two 8 inch (20 cm) round pans,
greased and lined with parchment (baking paper).

Bake in a moderate oven (350°F/180°C/Gas Mark 4) for 25–30
minutes, or until cooked (test by pressing gently with a finger — if the
surface springs back it is cooked). Cool on a wire rack.

Split each cake carefully in two, then layer with Chantilly Cream and
strawberries. Decorate the top with piped whipped cream and whole
strawberries.

Serves 8

Strawberry Sorbet with Cookie Hearts

½ cup (4 oz/125 g) superfine
  (caster) sugar
½ cup (4 fl oz/125 ml) water
2 punnets (approximately 1 lb/500 g)
  strawberries, hulled

1 teaspoon balsamic vinegar
extra strawberries, to serve

SORBETS used to be served as a palate cleanser between courses, but now the trend is to serve them as a delectably light dessert. Balsamic vinegar brings out the taste of strawberries to perfection.

Put the sugar, water, strawberries and vinegar into a food processor or blender and purée until the sugar is dissolved.

Pour into a shallow container and put into the freezer. After the sorbet starts to freeze (about 1 hour) take it out of the freezer occasionally and use a fork to break up any large crystals that form.

Serve in glasses or bowls with Cookie Hearts.

Serves 4

COOKIE HEARTS

•

6 oz (180 g) butter
¾ cup (6 oz/180 g) sugar
1 egg
1 tablespoon milk
1 teaspoon vanilla extract
  (essence)
10 oz (300 g) all-purpose
  (plain) flour, sifted
¾ teaspoon double-acting
  baking powder (1 ½
teaspoons baking powder)

•

Cream the butter and sugar. Add the egg, milk and vanilla. Add the dry ingredients and combine well. Chill for 1 hour. Roll out the dough and cut heart-shaped cookies. Put on greased baking sheets and bake for 10 minutes at 350°F (180°C/Gas Mark 4).

•

Tamarillos Poached in Red Wine with Blackberry Sauce

2 cups (16 fl oz/500 ml) red wine
½ cup (4 oz/125 g) sugar
1 vanilla bean
4 large tamarillos (or fresh peaches can be used)

8 oz (250 g) blackberries, fresh or frozen
Individual Meringues, for serving

FOR perfect poached fruit handle with care and turn occasionally in the syrup to keep the tone even.

Put the red wine, sugar and vanilla bean into a saucepan and bring to a simmering point, stirring to dissolve the sugar. Add the fruit and cook gently until tender but keeping their shape (about 15 minutes), turning occasionally in the syrup. Cool in the liquid.

Using a slotted spoon, transfer the tamarillos to another bowl and carefully peel off the skin. Pour the syrup into a saucepan. Add the blackberries to the saucepan, bring to simmering point and continue cooking for 5 minutes. Remove the vanilla bean. Serve with the poached tamarillos and meringues.

Serves 4

INDIVIDUAL MERINGUES

•

4 egg whites
pinch cream of tartar
1 cup (8 oz/250 g) sugar

•

Beat the egg whites with the cream of tartar until soft peaks form. Gradually add the sugar, beating until thick and glossy. Line baking sheets with parchment (baking paper). Roughly shape individual meringues on the sheets. Bake in a slow oven (250°F/130°C/Gas Mark ½) for about 1½ hours, or until the meringues are crisp and pale brown. Leave in the oven to cool.

•

Tiramisu

1 lb (500 g) mascarpone
4 oz (125 g) confectioners' (icing)
   sugar
3 egg yolks, beaten
3 egg whites
2 plain sponge cakes, cut into
   rectangular slices

½ cup (4 fl oz/125 ml) strong black
   coffee
½ cup (4 fl oz/125 ml) Tia Maria
chocolate, grated

COMBINE the mascarpone and sugar then stir in the egg yolks.

In a separate bowl, beat the egg whites until soft peaks form, then fold into the mascarpone mixture.

Put a layer of sponge slices into a glass bowl and sprinkle with strong black coffee and Tia Maria.

Spread some mascarpone mixture over the sponge layer, then continue layering slices of sponge sprinkled with coffee and Tia Maria with the mascarpone mixture, finishing with a layer of mascarpone. Refrigerate overnight.

Just before serving sprinkle with grated chocolate.

Serves 8

Tulips of Avocado Icecream

4 oz (125 g) confectioners' (icing)
   sugar
4 oz (125 g) butter, softened
4 egg whites

4 oz (120 g) all-purpose (plain)
   flour, sifted
Avocado Icecream, for serving
macadamia nuts, chopped

BEAT together the sugar and butter until creamy. Add the unbeaten egg whites and flour and mix to a paste.

Roll the paste out on a floured work surface and cut into six circles about 4 inches (10 cm) in diameter. Transfer to greased baking sheets with room in between to allow for spreading. Bake in a hot oven (400°F/200°C/Gas Mark 6) for 8–10 minutes or until the circles are golden brown around the edges.

Use a spatula to remove the circles from the baking trays and drape each one over a wide-brimmed glass or a small bowl so that it cools into a tulip shape.

When cool and set in a tulip shape, store in an airtight container. To serve place a scoop of Avocado Icecream in each tulip and sprinkle with nuts.

Serves 6

AVOCADO ICECREAM

•

1 avocado, halved and deseeded

juice of 2 limes

4 tablespoons confectioners' (icing) sugar, sifted

approximately 16 fl oz/ 500 ml vanilla icecream, softened

•

Scrape the pulp out of the avocado halves and mash, then mix in the lime juice and the sugar. Fold the avocado mixture into the softened icecream and return to the freezer to refreeze

•

White Chocolate Mousses

6 oz (180 g) semi-sweet (dark)
    chocolate, chopped
4 oz (125 g) white chocolate,
    chopped

4 eggs, separated
⅛ cup (1 fl oz/30 ml) Cointreau
white chocolate, grated

INDIVIDUAL white chocolate mousses look — and taste — great served in dark chocolate cases.

Melt the dark chocolate by stirring in a bowl over hot water.

Put twelve paper patty cake cases in a muffin pan. Divide the melted chocolate between the paper cases and use the back of a teaspoon to spread the chocolate evenly over the sides and base of the paper cases. Chill in the refrigerator until the chocolate hardens.

Melt the white chocolate by stirring in a bowl over hot water. Remove from the heat and stir in the egg yolks and the Cointreau.

In a separate bowl, beat the egg whites until soft peaks form, then fold them into the white chocolate mixture.

Peel the paper carefully off the dark chocolate cases. Spoon the white chocolate mousse mixture into the chocolate cases.

Refrigerate for at least 1 hour before serving. Decorate with grated white chocolate curls.

Makes 12

Index